Of Ash

& Auroras

RYAN MATTHEW TOOHER

OF ASH & AURORAS

IN LOVING MEMORY OF:

Christen M. Tooher

(21 May, 1989 - 24 Jan, 2023)

Of Ash & Auroras

Table of Contents:

To My Loving Wife Christy	2
Loves Timeless Embrace	4
I Deserve This	6
All But One	8
If Never Comes Again	10
Life's River	12
The Joke	14
Decay	16
Fragments	18
A Letter Of Love	20
IFILWY	22
The Rest Of My Life	24
Gothic Cathedral	26
It's Not A Game	28
Nostalgia's Reverie	30
Chandra: Pt 1	32
Chandra: Pt 2	34
Lodestone	36
The Aphonic Address	38
Implosion	40
The Garden Of Eggshells	42
A Quote	44
Embers	46
Incantation Of The Silent Grove	48
I Am Become The Egregore	50
About The Author & Acknowledgments	52

Of Ash & Auroras

Of Ash & Auroras

To my loving wife Christy

To my love, there are so many ways to tell of how I'm stricken with an unimaginable grief. But let me instead detail some of the myriad ways I'm thankful for the best 10 years of my life. Firstly, I am eternally thankful for being given the opportunity to share our lives with one another for the past decade. Our memories and the lessons that I've learned in those 10 years are boundless. You held my hand through all the difficult times and showed me how to be a better version of myself for others. You wrapped your arms around me and permeated my soul with love through the shaking fits of torment caused by PTSD. You've provided me with a sense of resolve when in uncertain situations. You lead me by example on how to be patient and take my time with anything that comes my way. Ya know, the army has certain core values that describe how a soldier operates. The acronym is LDRSHIP. Loyalty, Duty, Respect, Selfless service, Honor, Integrity, and Personal courage. These are values that you exemplified every single day, even having not been in the army. I admire the way you just innately embodied all these characteristics and lived them with grace, beauty, tenacity, snarkiness, and flair. You had this ethereal charm that no-one could quite explain. You had the quirkiest magnetic personality, whether it be your stoic mannerisms or infectious laugh. Your strong feminist fundamentals always left a lasting impression on myself, your friends, family, and strangers, and in a way, it imparted some of yourself to them. I am proud to be called your husband, and I'm proud of the person you are, not were. I feel you around me and in my head. I will carry you with me forever. I am thankful for the whole shebang dear. I love you wholly and eternally. Your loving hubbykins, Ryan. P.S. Anyone who knows you knows that French fries will always remind them of you. <3

Of Ash & Auroras

LOVES TIMELESS EMBRACE

Well, I asked you one night,
if you would mind being mine,
in a dream in my mind, at a time before time.
When light didn't exist, when we were all but a mist,
of pure energy and great masslessnesses.
You smiled at me, and then your eyes shown,
a light so bright, it couldn't be known,
You said yes to me, in that ethereal place,
of nondimensional limitless space.
We kissed by the starlight that had yet to shine,
And our love burned so bright, as if something divine.
We constructed our place, then created our time,
we then made our day, and our spirits entwined.
Our love was real and ever sublime
when two became one in that dream before time.
When all that was known, to be all it could be.
Our consciousnesses, and our Reality.
So may our love continue to grow and expand,
Beyond spatial conception, transcending times sand.
And though entropy will waste this natural plane.
One thing is for certain,
our love will remain.

Of Ash & Auroras

I Deserve This

I believe I deserve losing you.
And, it's going to keep on hurting because that's what it's meant to do.
I miss your smell, your laugh, your yell, your scream, your dreams.
You were everything to me,
Everything to me.
The days I face your lost embrace disgrace and race in my brain with haste,
and I'll try,
to learn to get up and fly or die cause I'd rather be high then a fucking waste.
I yearn for your voice, my comfort, my home.
This daily gut punch is getting old.
I never deserved your smiling eyes or kind touch,
or so,
to myself, I am told as much.
I woke up in hell the day that you died, but I deserve it for all the tears I made you cry.
I tried to save you from a thousand miles away, but by the time we knew what was happening,
it was already too late.
I believe I deserve losing you. It's going to keep on hurting because that's what it's meant to do.
But if I'm being honest,
I'm selfish,
So I don't want it to.

Of Ash & Auroras

ALL BUT ONE

I knew true love, in every way but one.
It was 10 whole years of marriage,
but it ended just as fast as it had begun.

We were kids when we met so many years ago.
We never did quite grasp where life would take us,
or which trail or path to go.

We thought we had time, like the seasons always turning,
Like the sun that sets but always rises, never something worth concerning.

Ten long years of love, of laughter, of growing side by side,
but forever slipped between the cracks, no matter how we tried.

I knew true love in every way but one.
The growing old together kind,
the one we never got to run.

Of Ash & Auroras

If Never Comes Again

I remember this one time you made a witty joke that took me over ten minutes to get.
You've shown your love for outer space and every single pet.
I remember watching fireworks in a great big sprawling crowd, and acting like we're alone with no one else around.
I'll never get to see you smiling next to me with friends. I'll never get to hear you say you're proud of me again.
All the happiness and tears and fears, and fun.
All the memories and things we've said and done.
You know they'll be guiding me back home like a shining light, and because of those bright beacons, I know that I will always be alright.
If never comes again.

Of Ash & Auroras

LIFE'S RIVER

This world,
this heart,
this existence,
is cracked in half upon the wilting petals of fragility.
The ebb and flow of life's river can be fast and strong, or soft and slow.
Rarely does it let you know that when you get in, it will move you.
Never were we given a choice to brave the river, and never will we reach the shore.
It's water, beguiling as it may be, is a treacherous deep.
Paddle as we may, we are still at the mercy of the unseen.
This river is pain,
this river is sweet,
this river is deep.

Of Ash & Auroras

The Joke

There's a joke I once heard, I forgot how it went.
Like something to do with the time we've all spent.
Circling the globe and then the sun too,
the joke escapes me, as I haven't a clue.
The joke talked of people and the lessons they learned,
the places they've been, and the money they've earned.
Pictures of happiness, heartache, and strife,
Ahh, now I remember the joke was called Life!

But jokes have a punchline, though there's none to be made...

DECAY

I'd give my life for you on my happiest day.
I'd sacrifice for you, my rights for you,
and leave what's left to
slowly decay.

Of Ash & Auroras

FRAGMENTS

People are like vases,
I don't want to rebuild your vase. I have my own
to worry about. I don't want to fit into yours, nor
do I want to put our broken pieces together to
build a complete one.
I want you to rebuild your broken self, and I'll do
the same.
We can then sit side by side atop the shelf of life,
sharing a space, but having our own.
We can sit there, being the gorgeous pieces of
art we are.

Of Ash & Auroras

A LETTER OF LOVE

Dear future love of my life,
This letter holds my hopes and dreams for the love we might share. I would love for our relationship to be built on open communication, a place where we can cooperate and
find strength in compromise.
I would love to create a space where kindness, compassion, and unconditional love are our guiding lights. A place where we can always find support and where forgiveness is a natural part of our bond. Honesty and loyalty will be the bedrock of our trust.
I want to fully respect ourselves and one another. I'd like us to extend that respect outward toward the world. I believe in personal growth and will celebrate your journey alongside my own.
I would love for us to be there for each other through the challenges life brings. I believe a clear determination and focus on love can overcome nearly anything. I know I'm not perfect, but I promise to always do my best. If these values resonate with you, perhaps together we can build a love that lasts a lifetime. With warmth and anticipation,
The future love of
your life.

Of Ash & Auroras

IFILWY

I'm falling in love with you but you may never know.

Crazy to think how emotions can flow.

Over and under like an invisible stream.

You could swim in it but it might never be seen.

The Rest of My Life

I could wake up next to you for the rest of my life,
as the things you see as flaws are simply traits in my eyes.
They are the things that make you human, the pains that make you live and grow.
And I know they're incredibly hard. But they are there to reveal or show.
Show you brightness in the other half of darkness that would swallow you whole if you let it.
To show you beauty in the cracks and crags of an old person's smile, You get it.
In my eyes, the traits you see as flaws tell of a burning passion for life becoming sharper and more salient too.
So yeah, I could wake up next to you for the rest of my life.
But could you?

Of Ash & Auroras

GOTHIC CATHEDRAL

You remind me of a Gothic cathedral in the
middle of the night, when a light fog rolls in.
And it's not just your outer beauty, but what's
enchanting lies within.
Illuminated by the moonlight shining through
the stained glass up above.
I want to explore every detail, every secret you
hold, my love. Bask in its pale glow as we share
are deepest, darkest desires, until we cry with
lust so loudly,
into the night so resoundly,
that people fear our fire.

It's Not A Game

I see your pain and hurt and torment,
and I raise you light, love, and companionship.
Light to illuminate your soul, to guide my love to those
open, weeping places that sorrowfully ache.
Love to flush and heal the damage done by the fake
kings, hateful queens, and treacherous k/nights.
A love pure enough to bear as a standard in the cosmic
specimen jar of the celestials.
A love that's co-creative with companionship, feeding,
and filling our lives with splendor.
Companionship to keep your mind safe from torment,
where echoes of their deceit fade.
A safe haven where memories of false promises yield to
the warmth of a genuine bond.
A fortress woven from indestructible shared
experiences and silken whispers of hope will stand
against the darkness.
Here, your wounds from your trials will mend,
and with some nurturing,
a bond of love will be forged into the winning hand.
I'm all in...

Of Ash & Auroras

Nostalgia's Reverie

I remember a time, when I was younger, when I'd race the twilight to the shore.
Back then, it was a free ride, chasing nights with twinkling lights at their core.
Nostalgia can hurt your soul, thinking about moments you regret, never again being able to experience those times you can't forget.
But moreover, it can heal you, with memories full of love, and the pieces come together into a peace and joy thereof.
I remember dancing carefree and absorbing all the fun, where hours morphed to minutes just seconds before the sun.
Those times were some of my favorite blissful memories.
And that's the how and why and what brings about nostalgia's reverie.

Chandra Pt 1

Pierce the cantankerous void and shine into the wandering eye of the traveler, purloining their gaze as you have done on innumerable occasions before. Your visage is that of lithic, ethereal beauty, ever present, ever guiding.

Permeate the quiet, tenebrous vacuum and glow over every little nuanced thing before you. Cast your pale lux upon the slumbering world, tracing spectral filigree along the undulating waves and the crested shadows of our forgotten terrain. A salient memoir of who else might have observed within their own ephemeral sliver of existence.

How many weary souls have sought solace in your aura? How cacophonous their whispers must be, as their tribulations combined are spoken at once into the ineffable heavens.

Of Ash & Auroras

Chandra Pt 2

How many lost wanderers have found their path beneath your graceful dominion, their burdens momentarily lifted by your placid brilliance? You, who have borne witness to the ages, inscrutable, remain stalwart in your celestial setting. Grant me your soft, gentle touch once more, so that I may see what lies beyond that shadowy veil. Let your radiance fracture the umbral expanse, unveiling the occult topography, esoteric truths, and unknowable wonders.
Illumine the shrouded corridors of my mind and shepherd me through life's lacuna, so that I may glimpse the effulgent mysteries that dwell beyond the periphery of sight. A celestial constant,
My Chandra.

Of Ash & Auroras

LODESTONE

I am a lodestone for love and positivity.
I attract those who hone and own a sense of purpose and kindness.
I'll become the epicenter of something great and make the earth shake and quake beneath my steps quietly.
I'll create a life of stupendous bliss in those I trust with my heart.
Because,
Fairy tales do not exist, but I do.
I'm a fucking human too.
I have wants and needs and hopes and dreams,
Just like you.

Of Ash & Auroras

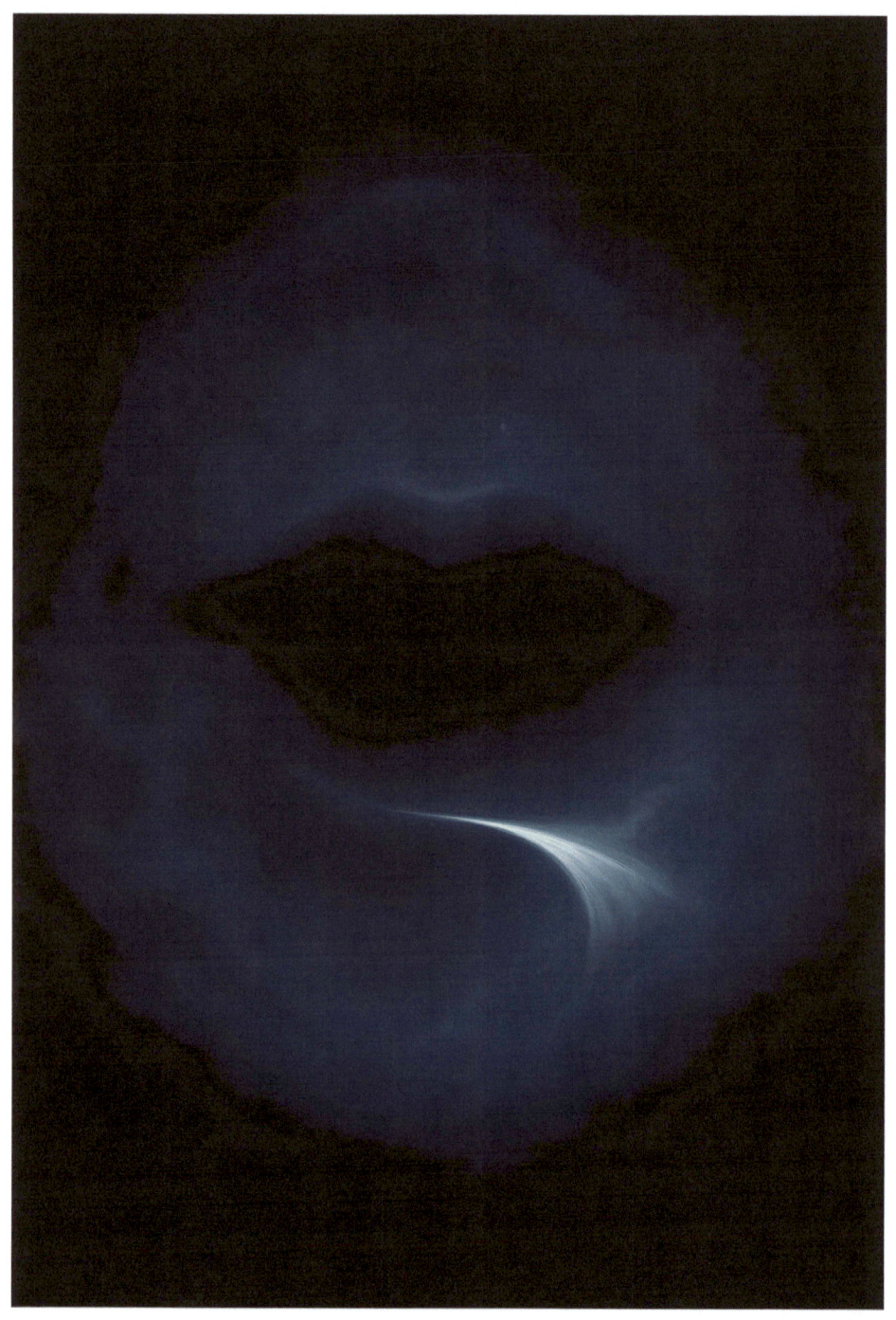

The Aphonic Address

Your quietude is an abyss,
a void where your voice should resonate.
Each echo of an unregarded utterance dissolves
its hope into a frigid hush.
The strength to transform this silence lies with
you, to offer a word, a bridge across the vast
chasm.
Yet, you choose to withhold, leaving me
suspended in the gravitational well of your
absence.
This deafening nothing seeps into my mind,
distorting my clarity with an aural fog.

Of Ash & Auroras

Implosion

I want to scream a hole into spacetime,
blasting the fundamental forces apart into an entropic nothingness.
To the point at which the observer can no longer bear witness to or even have the most quantum level of knowledge of the fact that they ever had an existence.
Shrieking sweet nothings like Gama ray bursts into the vestibules of our causal reality.
Piercing the superior dimensions and devouring matter,
reality, and consciousness as a metaphysical strange matter.

Of Ash & Auroras

The Garden Of Eggshells

I don't walk on eggshells,
I crush them beneath my feet to nourish the earth.
From the fertile soil, a breathtaking garden shall bloom.
The garden's roots run deep,
interweaving with the shattered fragments,
drawing sustenance from past fragility.
The air hums with the buzz of pollinators,
the beating of their wings, like those of war drums,
is a proclamation of power.
Thorns protect the delicate petals, like armor protects knights, a reminder that vulnerability can coexist with valor.
This Eden is a testament to transformation,
a sanctuary of steadfast spirit.
A kingdom of courage.

Of Ash & Auroras

A QUOTE

I owe myself my life,
but I'll never take it.

Of Ash & Auroras

EMBERS

In twilight hours when the shadows grow, and the dimming light begins to wane,
Don't succumb to life's sorrow, but rise against the dying flame.
Though time may weaken, our spirit's strong, don't let your inner fire cease,
Fight against the fading song, and find new strength through inner peace.
For in the depths of every soul, A spark of vibrant life resides, the torch that burns lights tales untold, like the light behind your eyes.
Embrace the moments with hearts ablaze, and a mind that's salient and serene,
For in the light that disappears, A new dawn can be seen.
Don't let darkness claim your day, but stand above the fading light, and when the embers fade away,
Find the courage to
ignite.

Of Ash & Auroras

Incantation of the Silent Grove

In the blackest depths, the old trees sway,
As I call to the night, from the end of the day.
By the breath of the earth and its whispered kin,
Let the moon's veil part, and the work begin.
O spirits of lost, hear my demand,
Arise from its roots, and take back this land.
With blood of black and eyes of flame,
Climb up from the deep well now to reclaim.
O creatures and plants, flora and fawn,
Come forth to me now in the name of Arawn.
By the might of his crown and stasis abound,
Let souls garner power, devour, and drown.
By the cut of the moonlight through the tops of the trees,
By the shadows that wisp along the night's breeze,
At the crossroads of life, the meniscus of mind,
Body and soul become intertwined.
So grant me your cosmic, ethereal power,
From all spectral realms of which we devour.
And bring the souls safe, back to whence they came,
Beyond the silent grove, all in your name.

Of Ash & Auroras

I Am Become The Egregore

We feel and heal and blend and mend,
and ebb and flow and stop and go,
in and out, and up and down,
and side to side and to and fro
and give and take, destroy and create,
burn and freeze in health and disease.
We see the blind and hear the deaf,
while screaming mute wails into depths.
We light the dark and darken the light
In this ever spiraling circle of life.
Ontological frameworks amorphous but single
Where fundamental forces become intermingled.
I've sought out the power we all stood to gain,
I've lived to infinities beyond what remained.
I shared in the all and what came before
now
I am become the egregore.

About the Author & Acknowledgements

Hi! I'm Ryan Matthew Tooher, and thank you for reading my book Of Ash & Auroras.
I'm writing in this format because I believe most authors' "About the Author" section to be pretentious.

I've lived a few different lives: soldier, survivor, widower, artist. None of them fit into a neat box, but that's what makes us all different.

I write because some things can't stay trapped inside, and poetry has always been a way of breaking the silence without physically screaming.

I grew up between two worlds, the bright lights of a childhood spent acting on Broadway, and the darker realities that came with war and loss later in life.

I served as a Cavalry Scout in F-Troop 1st CAV in the Army and deployed to Ramadi, Iraq, where I earned a Purple Heart and left with scars that don't always show.

I lost people I loved, including my late wife, Christy, and the echoing memories of that loss shape much of what I create today.

Writing, music, and art are how I keep moving forward and are an integral part of my healing journey.

Of Ash & Auroras

I believe in leaving the sugarcoating in life for pastry chefs of the world. Dressing up pain doesn't make it more palatable. If anything, my work is about finding meaning and value in the chaos of existence rather than despite it.

I believe in kindness, loyalty, and the simple principle of the golden rule.

I'm honored that you're here, sharing a piece of that journey with me.

Stay hydrated, my friends.

- Ryan

A super special thanks goes out to all my friends and family who have been there for me throughout the years.

In no particular order, the following people have helped to shape me into the person that I am today, and I want to acknowledge their efforts:
Christen Marie Tooher
Tom & Mary Woodward, Jerry and Marilyn Smedley, Dr. Tommy Woodward, Carey Sherman, Dave Smedley, Kellye Hogan, Daniel Corwin Ammentorp, The Donohue Family, CSM (Ret.) Daniel Pinion, and the men of F-Troop 1st CAV

Notes:

Notes:

Of Ash & Auroras

Credits:

Illustrated via extensive prompting utilizing AI tools and countless hours of meticulous image manipulation and editing by Ryan Matthew Tooher.

Authored, compiled, edited, produced, and published by Ryan Matthew Tooher.

For more of my creations,
Please Visit:
Http://www.fantomzap.com/

www.ingramcontent.com/pod-product-compliance
Lightning Source LLC
Chambersburg PA
CBHW041404090426
42743CB00006B/148